# Just Like Me!

## A Book About
## A Girl with a Rare Disease

by Anne Rugari

Printed in the United States of America
Published by Braughler Books LLC., Springboro, Ohio

First printing, 2018

ISBN: 978-1-945091-93-3 soft cover
ISBN: 978-0-9822187-1-6 hard cover

Library of Congress Control Number: 2018954041

Ordering information: Special discounts are available on quantity purchases by bookstores, corporations, associations, and others. For details, contact the publisher at:

sales@braughlerbooks.com
or at 937-58-BOOKS

For questions or comments about this book, please write to:

info@braughlerbooks.com

Braughler™
Books
braughlerbooks.com

*Just Like Me!* was written to help all children understand that boys and girls with any rare disease are just like them. They may look different or act different, but inside they are just kids, like them. Hopefully the book will help encourage understanding of all children who are differently-abled. Such an important life lesson!

The little girl in this book was inspired by Gina Rugari. Gina was diagnosed with Krabbe disease, a leukodystrophy, just weeks after she was born. Her journey to high school was filled with joy, laughter, tears, struggles, and so many accomplishments. She loved crazy painted finger nails, Girl Scouts, and watching American Idol. She made art, played soccer, and was great on the computer. Even though she continued to lose muscle control and finger dexterity during her life she became a wonderful teacher. She was a lesson in love, bravery, and persistence for so many classmates, teammates, friends and adults.

Gina's smile could light up a room. Please use the story in this book to give your smile away to someone who may be different in some way, but is Just Like YOU!

A little girl named Gina has a rare disease. There are thousands of boys and girls of all ages in the United States and all over the world who have a rare disease! Gina has Krabbe disease which makes her slowly lose muscle and nerve control all over her body.

Girls and boys with rare diseases often spend a lot of time visiting the doctor or the hospital. It makes them scared and tired. The nurses and doctors are nice. They make visiting the doctor less scary and more fun.

The big yellow school bus is FUN! Gina loves getting on the bus with all of her friends. Sometimes it takes boys and girls a little longer to get on the bus because of a disease. Wheelchairs aren't scary! They are FUN.

Gina LOVES when her friends help her. They carry her school bag, hold her hand, and talk to her on the school bus. Gina's service dog, Bella, always waits at the bus stop too!

Gina loves school! Sometimes it's a little harder for children with a rare disease to get their school work completed. Gina has an educational assistant to help her. Gina has lots of ideas to share with her teacher

and classmates. She uses a communication device to share her ideas. Gina is so proud of her work and so is her mom. Her school work and artwork are always displayed at home so everyone can see.

Gina loves to be on stage! Even though Gina is in a wheelchair, she can dance and sing with everyone else. She smiles so big when people clap for her! Gina likes to dress up for plays just like all the other kids. Sometimes she is a little shy because she feels different, but all of her friends make her feel like she's an important part of the show. Gina has been in many school plays and a member of the school choir. It's very FUN to be performing on stage.

Gina has trouble breathing and sometimes her muscles are very sore from being in her wheelchair. When kids with a rare disease are at home, they often need help with medicines and special treatments. Gina has super nice caregivers to help with her treatments and medicines. The medicines help Gina breathe and relax so she can get a good night's sleep. Gina's dog Bella always sleeps with her. It makes Gina feel better. When Gina is awake she likes to hang out in her room, sing, look at all of her posters, play with her stuffed animals, and work on projects.

Just like all the girls, Gina LOVES to have sleepovers. She's invites friends from Girl Scouts and friends from school. Gina's favorite thing to do on weekends is to get her fingernails painted. They are long and fancy.

She has pictures put on them: footballs, scary witches, and snowmen. At the party, the girls play music, games, watch movies, and eat lots of snacks. Gina has a service dog! All the girls love Bella.

Gina loves to travel! She especially likes to go on vacation with her mom to the beach. Gina loves tubing on the back of the boat! Gina has a special wheelchair that helps her move through the sand. She builds sandcastles and likes to collect shells. Gina loves to swim because she can move freely in the water. She can hold her breath when she is under water. Gina likes to pretend she's a mermaid when she is swimming!

Gina loves to play soccer. It's a special kind of soccer called wheelchair soccer. Gina can go fast in her wheelchair. She can move the ball with her feet and wheelchair to score points. Gina even won a trophy playing wheelchair soccer! After the game the kids love to race each other around the field.

Gina's school planned a Homecoming dance. This is a dance you go to in high school and the whole school usually attends. The gym is decorated with balloons, lights, and fun decorations all around the room. There are snacks and drinks for everyone to have. A DJ or disc jockey plays fun music for everyone to dance to. All of the boys and girls dress up for the dance. Gina went shopping with her mom and bought a fancy, new dress to wear. She wore makeup and jewelry to the dance and fixed her hair in a pretty style. Gina knew it was going to be a lot of fun and was eager to go to the Homecoming dance. Gina loved being on the dance floor in her wheelchair. She was spinning all around the room and holding hands with her friends while they all danced together. Have you ever seen anyone dance in a wheelchair?

Gina has so many friends! They are all different colors and all different shapes. Everyone has something special about them. Most of Gina's friends are strong and healthy. Some of her friends have rare diseases and some are differently-abled. Gina was a friend to everyone.

Other friends at her school, or at yours, might have a rare disease. But inside they are just boys and girls. Gina likes to tell them, "You're Just Like Me!"

**Rare Diseases** affect one-in-ten Americans, in 7,000 different forms. Thirty-million people live with serious, lifelong rare conditions. The last day of February each year is dedicated as **Rare Disease Day**, which brings awareness to rare diseases all over the world.

**Krabbe Disease** (crab-ay,) also known as Globoid Cell Leukodystrophy, is a rare genetic disorder affecting the central and peripheral nervous systems. Progression of the disease is rapid and children typically die within the first few years of life. The only treatment currently available is an umbilical cord or bone marrow transplant.

## The Dunedin Fine Art Center
## Dunedin, Florida

The art featured in this book was created in the **Sketch Paint & Brush** class with Joy Ames and **Teen Drawing** class with Todd Still at the Dunedin Fine Art Center (DFAC). For over 40 years, DFAC has been offering exciting art opportunities in a most welcoming kind of way.

Visit online at www.dfac.org

## DFAC Youth Artists

### Sketch, Paint & Brush Class

Teacher: Joy Ames
Teen Assistant: Olivia Mikkelsen
Artwork: School Bus, Beach Scene, and Soccer

STUDENTS:

Jakks Fitzgerald, age 7
Addison Hornbaker, age 7
Adrianna Pignato, age 8
Ariana Hooker, age 10

### Teen Drawing Class

Teacher: Todd Still

STUDENTS:

Jessica Bennett: Talent Show and Classroom scenes
Thad Muchnok: Cover and Doctor's office
Eliana Smith: Homecoming Dance and Back Cover
Ashely Williams: Sleepover and Nighttime scenes

## About the Author

While raising her healthy first son, Philip, Anne Rugari lost a second son, Nick, to Krabbe disease in 1987. He was only a year old when he passed away. Anne knew, as she expected her third child in 1999, that the baby should be tested at birth for Krabbe disease, a genetic disorder. Baby Gina tested positive and received an umbilical cord blood transplant at just three weeks of age to give her the missing enzyme she needed to thrive. Gina Rugari was a pioneer in the Krabbe world of medicine and research and considered a miracle child. She lived to the age of fifteen, 14 years longer than her brother, Nick. During her lifetime, she couldn't walk and used a computer to talk, however, Gina was cognitively appropriate at every age. Gina attended school through her freshman year of high school, participated in her community, enjoyed swimming, travelled all over the country and was proud to be a Girl Scout for 10 years of her life. As her disease progressed to her peripheral nervous system, Gina lost her battle with Krabbe in the summer of 2015. From Anne's experiences with Krabbe disease and the loss of two of her three children she has used her talents to create awareness and advocacy about this rare disease. Anne founded Partners For Krabbe Research in 2012, has written and published her first children's book, co-founded a second non-profit for Krabbe disease in 2017, and is currently writing a more comprehensive book about her life with Gina and Nick. Anne supports research by funding and working with scientists, researchers and clinicians all in the hope of changing the outcome of people and families affected by this rare disease.

Anne Rugari with Nick and Gina

CPSIA information can be obtained
at www.ICGtesting.com
Printed in the USA
BVHW021447100119
537455BV00003B/5/P